T0023800

# Our Shining Flower

The fantastic journey to the Land of Tien Shan, to the Mountain of the Children, to our beloved daughter Shining Flower.

# Our Shining Flower

by
Dianna Smith

illustrations by Louise "Vibrant" Hughes

Our Shining Flower
by Bellavia Smith

© 2007 by Dianna Smith

For information on obtaining permission for reprints and excerpts, please contact
D. Smith
264 Washington Place
Hasbrouck Heights, NJ 07604

ISBN: 978-0-9797651-0-0

Edited by Patricia Lynn Reilly
All illustrations by Louise "Vibrant" Hughes
Cover design by Sally Ann Kueker
Interior design and typesetting by Sally Ann Kueker
of Zaneta Publication Design, Hudson, Iowa

Printed and bound by Walsworth Publishing Company
Marceline, Missouri in the United States of America

a gift of love and celebration
for our daughter

Once upon a time, a beautiful baby girl was born in the Land of the Tien Shan. Her land is filled with deserts and mountains. The mountains are steep and jagged, majestic in height, powerful in strength. In the winters, they are covered with a blanket of deep snow. During the spring and summer, the deserts of the land come alive and bloom with bright color.

When people looked at the baby girl, they gasped with delight so she came to be called Shining Flower. The night sky is vast in Shining Flower's part of the world. Thousands of stars light the sky and the moon bathes the desert in soft white light. On the night of Shining Flower's birth, the stars twinkled brighter than ever before welcoming her into the world. Those who attended her birth placed red velvet slippers embroidered with gold thread upon her feet.

Far over the sea from Shining Flower's land stands the Kingdom of the Source of All Love. Only those with pure hearts know of this Kingdom. Many ships pass by its shores without seeing it, for the Kingdom is invisible to their eyes. One hears rumors though of a troubled sailor here and there, on deck gazing upon the beauty of the rising sun, in awe of creation for one special moment, whose sadness dissolves in the shadow of this magical Kingdom.

Farther away still from Shining Flower's country of mountains and deserts is the land of King Rowland and Queen Lenora. This land is dotted with farmland and gentle rolling mountains covered with tall green trees. An important river borders the land to the east beginning its flow as a small stream to the north, gradually widening to support the ships bringing supplies and treasures from other lands.

On the western edge of King Rowland and Queen Lenora's Kingdom stands a forest. Strange sounds and cries can be heard from within this forest. They echo through the night sky above the Kingdom. It is not wise for anyone to go into the forest alone. The Evil Wizard Romnik lives in the darkest corner of the forest. At the base of a dying tree, long hidden from human eyes, is a spear. The tree is his home; the spear is the tip of the roof. Pity the human who wanders into Romnik's portion of the forest, they are never heard from again.

King Rowland and Queen Lenora live in a beautiful castle. It sits upon a hill surrounded by ribbons of lilies and golden flowers winding gently up to the castle doors. The King and Queen love each other very much. They met long ago when Lenora's friend, Princess Ann, invited her to attend a grand banquet.

The banquet was held in King Rowland's castle. The two girls laughed and giggled as they ate the food, listened to the musicians, and watched the jugglers and clowns. They caught glimpses of King Rowland. He was a happy man with an easy laugh. He entertained family and friends with stories and magic tricks. He became King at a young age when his parents died. Yet King Rowland could not find a Queen to share his Kingdom. No woman loved the

land with its rolling hills and flowing rivers as much as he did.

Later in the day, Princess Ann introduced Lenora to King Rowland at the banquet. The moment their eyes met and Lenora offered her hand to him, they both knew in their hearts that they would marry. Lenora loved Rowland's strong hands and deep voice. She loved to meet his eyes with hers. She loved his easy laugh, his stories, and magic tricks. Rowland loved Lenora's books and poetry, and her delight in the trees and ponds, fields and skies of the Kingdom. He loved to behold the light in her eyes and the smile in her heart, drawing others toward her to listen to what she had to say about matters great and small.

The Evil Wizard Romnik saw how much Rowland and Lenora loved each other and he was very jealous of their love. When Romnik was a very young man, he believed that all the young women in the Kingdom wanted to be his bride and indeed, many did. Each time one agreed to marry him, he became bored and sought a more beautiful bride. At last, he set his eyes and heart upon Lenora. Romnik did everything he could to win her heart. He lavished her with gifts and flowers. She returned them all.

The years went by and Romnik became obsessed with winning Lenora. His obsession turned his heart to the Source of All Evil, who gave Romnik many powers. The more Romnik used his powers, the less desirable he became. When Romnik heard that Lenora had fallen in love with King Rowland, he doubled his efforts to win her. Romnik did not know that Lenora was protected by the Source of All Love and that wizardry could not harm her. As Romnik cast spell after spell to no avail, his heart grew colder and colder.

On the day of the royal wedding, Romnik cast one great spell upon the couple: "Love so pure as shown by thee shall never find its way to three. Two you shall always be because Lenora's heart would not love me." The royal couple did not know that on their day of greatest joy such a wicked spell had been cast.

As the years went by, Queen Lenora became very sad because they did not have a child to love. The King understood how brokenhearted the Queen was. He consulted many royal advisors to discover a way to end her sadness, but nothing worked. The Queen's sadness began to cast a shadow on the light in her eyes and the smile in her heart.

One day, at a royal banquet, the King and Queen watched a little girl dance and laugh through the great hall. She had big blue eyes and jet-black hair. Tiny stars covered

her swirling dress and golden stars circled her head. Upon her feet were red velvet slippers embroidered with gold like those given to Shining Flower at her birth.

The little girl was from the Mountain of the Children. From the moment of her birth, the Mountain Elves, who protect the children, knew she had special gifts. Her life was dedicated to the Source of All Love. She traveled far and wide to shine her gift of joy and laughter into the sad hearts and homes of those absent of children's laughter.

The King watched the Queen smile as the little girl danced. He wanted to know more about her. He asked banquet guests about her, but no one had answers for him.

When the little girl came close, King Rowland realized this was no ordinary child; this was a fairy! The King spoke, "Little fairy, where are you from? . . ." The little fairy laughed a big smiling laugh, "Oh great King, I am from the far away land of Tien Shan. I was born in the Mountain of the Children." "Little fairy," asked the King, "why are you here, so far away from your land?"

"I come to bring you wonderful news. A baby girl has been born; she waits for you and your Queen even now." The King was not sure what to make of this report from the fairy. He and his Queen had been made many promises over the years in their quest to bring children into the joy they knew.

"Fairy," he said in disbelief, "are you tricking me?"

"No, great King, I would not trick you. Listen to my secret. Romnik, the powerful Wizard, jealous of the love you share with Queen Lenora cast a spell upon you on the day of your royal wedding. But, the Source of All Love is more powerful than the Evil Wizard's spell. Your Princess was born in the Land of Tien Shan, high in the Mountain of the Children. She is wrapped in the arms of Source of All Love, hidden from all danger."

The King could not believe his ears. Could this be true? The King asked the fairy to come with him at once to tell the Queen the secret.

"Oh no, great King, only you can tell the Queen. Because your love is strong, you will overcome all the challenges Romnik will put in your way until, at last, you and your Queen will hold the Princess in your arms."

And, with that, the fairy disappeared! How was the King to explain all this to his Queen? He prayed to the Source of All Love for wisdom to know what to say and how to say it.

The royal banquet continued. Many friends of the King and Queen came and went. The Duke and Duchess Brogan arrived. They were old, dear friends of the King, whom he had not seen in many years. He was overjoyed to greet them.

"Dear friends, how wonderful it is to see you after all these years," said the King.

_____

_____

_____

"Ah yes, my good friend, and I have a surprise for you, meet my family." And, he waved his hand to invite the Duchess and their three children to come near.

"Your Majesty, may I introduce my children."

Three little girls smiled up at King Rowland. He immediately got down on one knee to shake their hands and welcome them to the party! "Have a wonderful time, children, and ask my dessert chef to fill your plates with luscious delicacies."

King Rowland asked the Duke to tell him about his growing family. "Well, my friend, it has indeed been a long time since last we visited. As you know, the Duchess and I had met in our later years and while we were very happy together, we missed the love of children. He told the King how the Duchess was visited by a messenger who came in the form of a fairy. This fairy told of the Source of Love and the Tien Shan.

The King laughed and clapped his hands, "Thank you for sharing your secret" he cried with joy, "You see, for many years my Queen and I have also desired to share our love with a child. This very night the same fairy told me that our daughter had been born in the Land of Tien Shan. I didn't know whether to believe her. Others have taken advantage of our longing and caused us great disappointment. You have confirmed the truth of the fairy's words. Thank you!"

As he and his family were leaving, the Duke blessed the King and Queen with these words, "May the Source of All Love shine on your journey."

King Rowland immediately told the Queen about his conversation with the Duke. They vowed to go to the Land of the Tien Shan!

Meanwhile the little Princess, Shining Flower, was growing more beautiful every day. She played in the colorful gardens that surrounded her home, following the garden paths, exploring the stone fountains, and splashing in their waters. Loving spirits gave her everything she needed — food and clothing, a warm bed in the winter and cool breezes in the summer. The little girl smiled at everyone she met — yet deep in her heart she longed for a home with a mother and father of her own.

Shining Flower's first mother and father, whom she did not remember, had been poor farmers unable to get help when they fell ill. They both loved Shining Flower very much. Knowing they would die soon, they made the long trip to the Mountain of the Children and asked the elves to care for their child. The elves welcomed Shining Flower and assured her mother and father that they would find loving parents to raise Shining Flower.

As Shining Flower walked through the gardens and forests of the Mountain of the Children, she saw deer, ducks, and great golden eagles. Her desire to be part of a family grew stronger as she watched the animal and bird families. She took care of this secret desire growing in the deepest part of her heart while remaining grateful to the wonderful elves who loved her with kindness.

The day following his conversation with The Duke and Duchess Brogan, King Rowland gathered advisors and assistants from near and far to chart their course to their daughter. One such advisor arrived at the palace with letters of royal recommendation. Her name was Sulana and she promised to help the Queen and the King find their way to the Land of Tien Shan.

Many days and nights were spent with Sulana consulting maps, learning languages, and mastering the necessary details for such a treacherous journey. Sulana was paid handsomely for her services. The King and Queen willingly shared their resources with anyone who would assist them.

One day Sulana approached the Queen, "Your Highness, I have worked on your behalf for six months.

There is one last step we must take and for this I will need an even larger chest of gold from your reserves."

Lenora was confused. "Sulana, the King and I have opened our home to you; we have shared the desires of our heart with you; and we have paid you handsomely for all that you have done. We are weary and wish to begin the journey to our daughter. When will your work for us be complete?"

Sulana responded, "Your Highness, my work for you is almost complete! One final task must be accomplished. A courier will come to the palace in my name. He must be given this parchment to ensure your safe passage to the Land of Tien Shan. One small matter remains; I must have a final installment of gold to assure the safety of my courier and to provide for my departure journey."

With this Sulana gave the parchment to Queen Lenora. "I must discuss this matter with the King, Sulana." That night when the Queen and King were alone, Lenora told Rowland about her conversation with Sulana. "Something is very wrong." Lenora said, "My trust in Sulana is dissolving." The King promised to make some inquiries to get to the bottom of Sulana's motives and intentions.

The investigation was carried out in secret. A woodsman, who regularly groomed the trees on the palace grounds, reported that about six months prior, he saw Romnik coming out of the forest. The woodsman turned

for a moment to wipe the sweat from his brow. When he turned back, instead of seeing Romnik, he saw a woman riding toward the palace on a dark horse. The description he gave of the woman fit Sulana perfectly. Other reports reached the palace linking Sulana to the Evil Wizard Romnik.

Finally, the courier arrived. Sulana brought him with her into the Great Hall to meet the King and Queen and to receive her final installment of gold. She did not know about the investigation nor did she know that the Wise Women of the Kingdom were hidden behind the royal throne. As Sulana approached the throne, the Wise Women chanted, "The Source of All Love sees beyond the mask you wear." With those words, Sulana dissolved, and standing before Lenora and Rowland was none other than Romnik! Confronted by the pure light of the Wise Women, his disguise could not survive. "Be gone," they ordered, and with that, Romnik vanished.

The King and Queen were glad that they had not fallen victim to Romnik, yet valuable time had been lost. The Wise Women of the Kingdom continued to support the King and Queen to find their way to the daughter, waiting for them in the Land of Tien Shan. The Wise Women took the King and Queen to meet The One Who Holds the Focus. She was the center of all understanding and would make clear the perfect path to take to reach their child.

The One Who Holds the Focus told the royal couple that they must prepare documents to send to the elves standing guard at the Mountain of the Children. The elves were the children's guardians. Only those with pure hearts would be allowed to visit with the children; only those who had been visited by the magic fairy would be allowed to receive a child into their lives. And so, the King and Queen sent many royal documents to the Mountain Elves, along with paintings to show the beauty of the Kingdom and to reveal the likeness of Lenora and Rowland.

The One Who Holds the Focus gathered the mapmakers of the land and chose the most crystal clear maps of them all, to guide the King and Queen to the land of Tien Shan, to the Mountain of the Children, to their precious daughter, waiting for them there. Once the correct maps were chosen, the people of the Kingdom gathered in the royal courtyard to send Lenora and Rowland on their way with prayers of blessing and shouts of joy.

The journey took many days yet the time seemed to pass as gracefully as the flight of the golden eagles soaring

above Lenora and Rowland's caravan. Their hearts were light and steady as they moved closer to their daughter... until at last they reached the Land of the Tien Shan. In the distance, they saw the Mountain of the Children and they followed its bright light right up to the gate. Confused about how to move beyond the gate and enter, an elf appeared before them.

"What is all this noise?" grumbled the elf.

"Who are you?" asked the King.

"I am Igor and you woke me up!"

Igor was no ordinary elf. In the Mountain of the Children, all the elves had responsibilities. Some were responsible to cool the children when the summer heat climbed the mountain. Others were responsible for the forest and the health of its inhabitants. Igor was the gatekeeper. He was taller than the other elves and as a child, he felt out of place because his feet were too big for his elf slippers, and his arms dangled out of the sleeves of his elf jacket. His mother reminded him that the Source of All Love had given him a special gift — he was careful and could not be easily tricked. This made him the perfect gatekeeper!

As Igor grew older, the other elves respected his knowledge and his height! Many times, he was called to the gate in the middle of the night to inspect the motives and intentions of those who wished entry. He developed a series of tests to weed out those who were not sent by the magic fairy. His first test was to reject anyone who appeared at the gate. Igor knew that those with true love, pure hearts, and noble intentions would not accept his "No." They would persevere with kindness until the words of the magic fairy were obeyed and they were allowed entry.

"Where is the Princess? We have come a long way through many difficulties. We were told she would be here," said King Rowland.

"She is not here. Come back tomorrow!" and Igor disappeared.

The King and Queen were so surprised that they could not speak. The Queen broke their silence, "Come, my King, one day will not make a difference, and we must gather clothing and gifts for the Princess." So all day and into the night, the King and the Queen assembled a great many gifts for the Princess. They had fun purchasing toys, games, and clothing for the little girl.

They slept well that night and rose as the very first rays of sunlight came into the morning. They returned to the gate bearing gifts. No one was there to greet them. The King spoke into the emptiness of the space, "It is tomorrow, where is our Princess? We cannot bear any more heartbreak. Please answer us!"

Igor, the elf, reappeared. "Delighted," he said. With those words, the King and Queen found themselves flying like the eagles that soared above their caravan. They flew above steep and jagged mountains, majestic in height, powerful in strength. In the distance, they saw expansive deserts alive and blooming with bright color. At last, they landed in front of an enchanted house.

"Wait here," commanded Igor as he entered the house. Gasping to catch their breath after that most amazing flight, the King and Queen wondered what other adventure awaited them on their way to the Princess.

Igor returned and ushered them into the house with such dignity that the King and Queen felt like children being ushered into the presence of royalty. Igor positioned Lenora and Rowland in front of a most beautiful little girl. She looked a lot like the magic fairy except her eyes were coal-black. She was wearing red velvet slippers embroidered with gold thread. Tiny stars covered her swirling dress and golden stars circled her head.

Igor announced, "King Rowland and Queen Lenora meet Shining Flower." In the silence, she looked at them from deep within her coal-colored eyes, asking her heart, "Is this my family?"

Meanwhile King Rowland's heart became overwhelmed with love for this child in front of him. He got down on his knees and held out his arms. Shining Flower looked toward Igor who smiled and nodded his head, and she knew the answer to her question.

Shining Flower ran into the King's arms. He picked her up and they all hugged — mother, father, daughter, and Igor! Everyone had tears of joy flowing from their eyes. In the laughter and the tears, in the hugs of welcome and the words of love, Romnik's evil spell was broken and the Source of All Love declared that this family would share never-ending love. And so, they did!

# Postscript:

This story, set as a fairy tale, tells of our adoption journey. It was written as a gift of love and celebration for our daughter, and as a gift of encouragement and support for those of you traveling your own path to the child of your dreams.

The journey to our precious Shining Flower was not an easy one, however, we feel connected to all that is good and pure in this world as we gaze upon her each and every day.

We thank our friends and neighbors who supported us as we prepared our hearts and home, gathered the paperwork, took some wrong turns, and eventually made the fantastic journey to the Land of Tien Shan, to the Mountain of the Children, to our beloved daughter Shining Flower.

Indeed the Source of Love continues to smile on our family!

# Acknowledgements —

We thank our friends and neighbors, especially the people of Prattsville and Jewett New York, who supported us as we prepared our hearts and home, gathered the paperwork, took some wrong turns, and eventually made the fantastic journey to the land of the Tien Shan.

# Advance Praise —

The story of Shining Flower will touch your heart and soul. You and your children will read her story again and again.
— Rev. Kristina D. Hansen, Woodbury United Methodist Church, Woodbury, CT

A heartfelt story presenting both the difficulties and joys of one family's adoption journey. Telling the whole truth adds to the book's power.
— **Gretchen W. Janssen**, D.Min., Executive Director of the Creative Living Counseling Center, Allendale, NJ

An engaging tale, thoughtfully done, that kept my interest throughout. The eye-catching illustrations pulled me into Shining Flower's world.
— **Rev. William Faulkner**, Pastoral Counselor, Wyckoff Health Care Center, Wyckoff, NJ